This book belongs to

_____

_____

Includes 2 each of 25 creepy and cute fantasy coloring images by Selina Fenech.

As an artist, color is a thing of magic in my life. Color creates shapes, forms, and feelings in the artworks I paint. Laying color onto a blank page is when I feel closest to true magic, when I feel happiest and most relaxed, and it's through what I create that I share my love of magic with the world. Through my coloring books I want to share that same magic with you.

The artworks in my books are based on my completed paintings, which I have painted over the last ten years as a professional artist. I have created the coloring designs to be a mix of intricate and detailed while still fun and accessible. There is something for lovers of meditative detail while simple enough to not be overwhelming for younger colorists.

When designing my books I decided to print them with two copies of each design, because as an artist I know there are always so many possibilities! I also wanted to give everybody the chance of a do-over with every design in case of an oops (as an artist I know that happens too!). Try a different medium, or a different colour scheme. Or share the magic with a friend, child, parent, or sibling. Because sharing your creativity and joy of color is the best magic of all.

See the colors the artist chose for her paintings at www.selinafenech.com

Faedorables - Cute and Creepy Coloring Book
by Selina Fenech
First Published September 2017
Published by Fairies and Fantasy PTY LTD
ISBN: 978-0-6480269-8-3

Using This Book

Turn off and move away from distractions. Relax into the peaceful process of coloring and enjoy the magic of these fantasy images.

Experiment! There is no right or wrong way to color, and with two of each image, there's no pressure.

This book works best with color pencils or markers. Wet mediums should be used sparingly. Slip a piece of card behind the image you're working on in case the markers bleed through.

Don't be scared to dismantle this book. Cut finished pages out to frame, or split the book in half where the second set of images start so you and a loved one can color together.

Never run out of fantasy coloring pages by signing up to Selina's newsletter. Get free downloadable pages and updates on new books at - selinafenech.com/free-coloring-sampler/

Share Your Work

Share on Instagram with **#colorselina** to be included in Selina's coloring gallery, and visit the gallery for inspiration.

selinafenech.com/coloringgallery

"Voodoo"

"A Spell of Threes"

"Brains"

"Dragon Queen"

"Chain of Skulls"

"Darkling"

"Electricity"

"Headless Horsewoman"

"Vampy Friends"

"Fading Away"

"Little Devil"

"Medusa"

"Melody Dark"

"Miss Muffet"

"Mummy's Curse"

"Nice Night for Flying"

"Night's Companions"

"Wolf Pack"

"Persephone and Cerberus"

"Pretty Dolly"

"Pumpkin Patch Cats"

"Putting You Back Together"

"Reaper"

"Siren Song"

"Witching Hour"

Second Set of Pages Begins Here

When designing my books I decided to print them with two copies of each design, because as an artist I know there are always so many possibilities! I also wanted to give everybody the chance of a do-over with every design in case of an oops (as an artist I know that happens too!). Try a different medium, or a different colour scheme. Create without fear! Or share the magic with a loved one. Because sharing your creativity and joy of color is the best magic of all. ~ *Selina*

"Voodoo"

"A Spell of Threes"

"Brains"

"Dragon Queen"

"Chain of Skulls"

"Darkling"

"Electricity"

"Headless Horsewoman"

"Vampy Friends"

"Fading Away"

"Little Devil"

"Medusa"

"Melody Dark"

"Miss Muffet"

"Mummy's Curse"

"Nice Night for Flying"

"Night's Companions"

"Wolf Pack"

"Persephone and Cerberus"

"Pretty Dolly"

"Pumpkin Patch Cats"

"Putting You Back Together"

"Reaper"

"Siren Song"

"Witching Hour"

About the Artist

As a lover of all things fantasy, Selina has made a living as an artist since she was 23 years old selling her magical creations. Her works range from oil paintings to oracle decks, dolls to digital scrapbooking, plus Young Adult novels, jewelry, and coloring books.

Born in 1981 to Australian and Maltese parents, Selina lives in Australia with her husband, daughter, and growing urban farm menagerie.

FAIRY
COMPANIONS
COLORING BOOK
SELINA FENECH

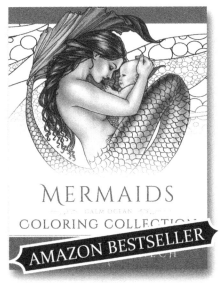

MERMAIDS
CALM OCEAN
COLORING COLLECTION
AMAZON BESTSELLER

GOTHIC
DARK FANTASY
COLORING BOOK
AMAZON BESTSELLER

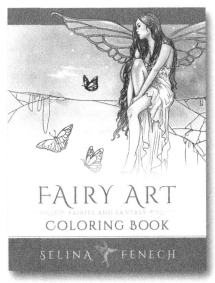

FAIRY ART
FAIRIES AND FANTASY
COLORING BOOK
SELINA FENECH

MAGICAL
MINIS
POCKET SIZED FAIRY FANTASY ART
COLORING BOOK
SELINA FENECH

ENCHANTED
MAGICAL FORESTS
COLORING COLLECTION
AMAZON BESTSELLER

See all books online at viewauthor.at/sfcolor

Share Your Work

Selina loves to see your finished designs and the colors you chose!
Share online with **#colorselina**

www.facebook.com/selinafenechart
www.selinafenech.com

Made in the USA
Columbia, SC
11 May 2020